EASY MEDITATIONS
for Grownups

30 ways to slow down
& calm your nervous system

Giselle Shardlow

KidsYogaStories.com
© Kids Yoga Stories

KIDS YOGA STORIES

www.KidsYogaStories.com

ISBN: 978-1-943648-51-1 (print)

Kids Yoga Stories
Boston, MA
www.kidsyogastories.com
www.amazon.com/author/giselleshardlow

Email us at info@kidsyogastories.com.

What do you think? Let us know what you think of *Easy Meditations for Grownups* at feedback@kidsyogastories.com.

Welcome to Easy Meditations
for Grownups

In these busy times, parents and teachers often feel overworked, underpaid (if they're paid at all), and undervalued. Creating your own calm and confidence through a regular, consistent breathing practice can make all the difference to your health and well-being. Getting back to the basics of using breath to reduce stress and anxiety allows us to be more available to our loved ones and our students. Remember that happy teachers and parents foster happy children!

Meditation has huge benefits, including:

- Increasing memory, focus, and attention
- Encouraging mindfulness and the ability to focus on the present moment
- Inviting long, deep breaths that calm the nervous system
- Providing time and space to quiet the mind and relax body
- Developing creativity and imagination
- Increasing emotional intelligence
- Reducing stress and anxiety

The meditation ideas in this book are broken down into three categories, or "anchors," in the index: breathing techniques, mantras, and focus. In meditation practice, it's important to have an anchor, like a ship in the water, to give us something simple and concrete to focus on. This anchor enables our minds to eliminate distractions and find calm.

1

Meditation Tips

- Start each meditation by coming to Resting Pose or choose another comfortable, relaxing position, such as sitting in a chair, sitting cross-legged, or sitting on your heels. Ensure that your spine is straight.

- Each meditation is designed to be practiced for about five minutes, but they are also great if you only have one minute or if you are at a point in your practice where you are ready to spend longer periods of time to sit silently.

- Each meditation invites you to close your eyes. However, if you are not comfortable closing your eyes, simply look down at a spot in front of yourself or stare at a candle flame.

- If you're wondering where to start, try beginning with the "Four Count" breath to get used to taking a deep breath in and a deep breath out. Remember that the simplest practices are often the most profound.

- Begin each meditation session by breathing naturally. Relax your body and calm your mind. Feel the benefits of slowing down and calming your mind.

- At the end of each meditation, when you're ready, return to breathing naturally and open your eyes. Notice any feelings or emotions you have about the meditation.

- The most important thing is to take a moment to pause and come to the present moment.

- These meditation pages are meant to inspire you with ideas, so feel free to make adaptations to suit your needs and preferences.

Meditation Tips

- Try practicing the meditations regularly to create a predictable and consistent ritual.

- Set up a special spot in your house or office to practice the meditations. Decorate the space with all your favorite things. Feel free to add your own props, music, or books to make the experience more meaningful and comfortable for you.

- Don't worry if the meditation experience doesn't meet your expectations the first time. Try again another time.

- Accept that your thoughts might wander and that's perfectly okay; just come back to your anchor and begin your practice again.

- Keep doing it. You'll hit the point when you'll feel the effects, and then there's no turning back. Watch for those miracles. You'll know when the moment comes. You'll feel a sense of peace.

- Notice that your calm and happiness has ripple effects to the children and adults in your life. Meditation is worth it.

- Be gentle with yourself. Your practice should be steady and joyful. Remind yourself that meditation is a lifelong practice and look for little miracle moments along the way.

- Feel free to ask someone to join you on your meditation challenge to hold each other accountable and share experiences.

- Remind yourself that the intention of meditations is to reduce your stress and anxiety and tune in more deeply to yourself. Then you will be better able to deal with the daily challenges that come your way.

Index

Index

Focus

Breathing Techniques

Belly Breath

Take a moment to sit silently in a quiet spot.

Place one hand on your belly and
the other hand on your chest.

Start to inhale, counting to four in your mind.

Then exhale, counting to four in your mind.

Feel the rise and fall of your breath
in your belly and chest.

Think of filling your belly
with air like a balloon.

Continue this belly breathing for
at least five minutes, if possible.

Box Breath

Sit in a comfortable position, breathing normally.

Then take a deep breath in for four counts.

Hold it for four counts and then exhale for four counts.

Hold your breath for four count and
then inhale for four counts.

Repeat the pattern of inhale-hold-exhale-hold,
visualizing your breath traveling around a square box.

Or you might even use your finger to trace
a square in the air as you breathe.

Continue like this for a few minutes
and then come to breathing naturally.

Count to Ten

Sit silently in a comfortable position,
breathing deeply.

Inhale for four counts and
then exhale for four counts.

On your next inhale-exhale,
count "One" in your head.

Then count all the way to ten
with each inhale-exhale.

If your mind wanders, don't worry.
Just come back to one and start again.

You could also use your fingers to help count to ten.

Extended Exhale

Bring attention to your breath.

As you inhale, count to four in your mind.

Then exhale slowly,
counting to eight in your mind.

Continue this breathing pattern
for a few moments.

If you need to take a break,
simply return to breathing naturally
then go back to the extended exhale
when you're ready.

15

Four Count

Come to sitting comfortably
in a cross-legged position or on a chair
with your feet firmly planted on the ground.

Place your palms face-up on your knees.

Close your eyes.

Breathe naturally, feeling the rise and fall
of your chest and belly.

You could keep your palms on your knees
or give yourself a bear hug by placing your right palm
under your left armpit and left palm
on your right shoulder.

Then, when you're ready,
start to take deeper breaths.

Inhale, counting to four in your head.

Exhale, counting to four in your head.

Continue like this in your relaxed position
or in your bear hug for a few minutes,
breathing in for four and out for four.

Mantras

Everything I Need
is Within Me

This mantra is perfect if you just need
a little boost of confidence.

Once you're settled into a quiet place,
sitting comfortably, with your palms in your lap,
breathe normally.

Then bring attention to your breath and
take a few deep inhales and exhales.

As you're sitting silently, taking deep breaths,
think to yourself, "Everything I need is within me."

As you think the words, imagine them draping over
your whole body, and believe in the words.

Let Go

Find a comfortable seated position with your feet on the ground and your spine straight.

Once you've settled in, bring your attention to your breath.

Start to go deeper and take deeper breaths.

Start to count to four as you inhale and exhale.

On your next inhale, think, "Let."

On your next exhale, think, "Go."

Continue with this breathing and mantra for at least five minutes.

If you get distracted, pull yourself back to your breath and this positive affirmation.

When you're exhaling with "Go," really think consciously of letting go of any mental or emotional stress or anxiety.

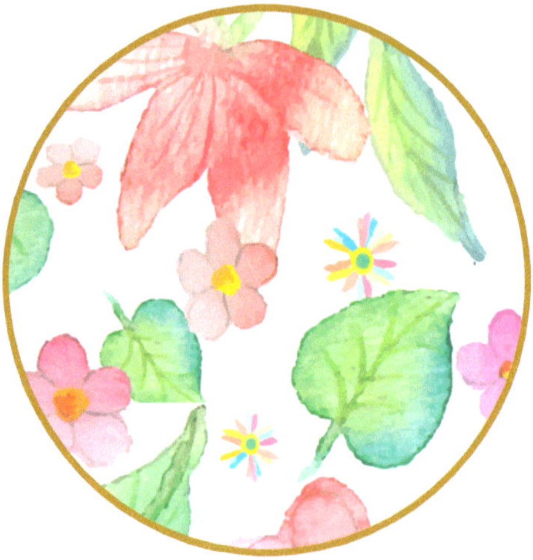

Peace-Love

Get into a comfortable seat and bring
your attention to your breath.

Inhale for four counts, thinking, "Peace."

Exhale for four counts, thinking, "Love."

Continue with this peace-love mantra
for at least five minutes.

You could even use this mantra throughout
the day, with your eyes open,
while doing things at home or at work.

Steady-Joyful

Come to sitting comfortably with a tall spine.

Take in a deep inhale for four counts
and then exhale for four counts.

On your next inhale, think, "Steady,"
followed by an exhale as you think, "Joyful."

Repeat the "steady" and "joyful" mantra
for at least five minutes.

I Am Calm

Once you are settled comfortably,
take a few moments to breathe normally.

In you inhale, think, "I am."

As you exhale, think, "Calm."

As you go through your "I am calm" mantra,
consciously think of calming each part
of your body, melting into the ground.

Calm your busy thoughts and
bring your focus to your mantra.

Believe in the words.

I Am Grateful

Come to sitting with a tall spine.

On a deep inhale, think, "I am."

On a long exhale, think, "Grateful."

Continue like this, thinking, "I am grateful"
for at least five minutes.

If your mind wanders, don't worry—
just bring it back to the mantra.

Surrender into your meditation.

Completely relax your mind and body
with each breath.

I Am Happy
and Healthy

Come to sitting comfortably with a tall spine.

Take in a deep inhale for four counts
and then exhale for four counts.

On your next inhale, think, "I am,"
followed by an exhale as you think, "Happy."

On your next inhale, think, "I am,"
followed by an exhale as you think, "Healthy."

Repeat these affirmations
for at least five minutes.

I Am Present Now

As you go through your meditation practice today,
think to yourself, "I am present now"
(or "I am here now").

Continually bring yourself back
to the present moment.

Let your worries, fears, and anxieties fall away.

Listen to your breath and think,
"I am present now."

Peace is in the present moment.

I Can Do This

Find a comfortable sitting position
and rest your palms on your knees.

Begin to take deeper inhales and longer exhales.

On an exhale, think, "I can."

On your next exhale, think, "Do this."

While you are going through this breathing mantra,
try smiling at the same time.

Feel the meaning of the words as you say them.

Feel the optimism.

You could also try saying, "Positive mind"
on the inhale and "Positive life" on an exhale.

I Love Me, You, and Everyone

Find a relaxed position with a tall spine and your palms on your knees.

On your deep inhale, think, "I love me."

Then exhale, thinking, "I love you."

Think of someone special.

Then, as you continue to inhale and exhale, think, "I love everyone."

Think of various people in your life.

Continue like this for at least five minutes.

Focus

Ask a Question

Find a comfortable sitting or lying position—
in a quiet place, if possible.

Rest your hands on your knees,
palms facing upward, and straighten your spine.

Bring your awareness to your breath,
feeling the expansion of your chest followed by
the release of air from your body.

Let a question come to your mind.
It could be something new or something that
has been ruminating in your mind for a while.

As you start to take deeper breaths,
bring your awareness to the sound of your breath.

Count to four as you inhale and count to four as you exhale.

Let your mind ponder your question.
See what comes up as your mind sifts through
various thoughts and ideas.

Keep breathing deeply as you continue to let
your mind linger on this question.

Don't force it. Just see what comes up.

Body Scan

Sit or lie down silently in meditation.

Breathe deeply in and out,
while scanning your body.

Think about each body part and relax it.

Start with your feet.
Bring your attention to your feet
and simply relax them.

Then relax your lower legs.

Next, relax your knees and
then your upper legs, your belly,
and your chest.

Next, think about your hands.
Relax your hands.

Then your elbows.
Then your arms.
Then your shoulders.

Now, think about your face.
Relax your face.
Then your chin.
Your mouth. Your nose.
Your eyes. And your head.

Feel the sensations and hear the
sounds that your body makes.

Send love and gratitude to your body.

Accept your body for what it is
and what it is not.

Calm Music

Find a quiet spot and put on
some calming music.

It could be your favorite music or something new,
just as long as it's calming.

As you begin your mindful breathing,
bring your attention to the music.

Get curious about the sounds of the music.
Can you hear specific instruments?
What might have inspired the musician?

Think about how the music makes you feel
as you take deep breaths in and out.

Let the music envelope you,
like a cozy blanket.

Far, Near, Inside

Sit comfortably in an upright position.

Take in a deep inhale and
then a long exhale,
each for four counts.

While you are breathing deeply,
start to listen for sounds that are far away
outside for a few minutes.

These sounds might come from outside,
such as the sounds of the street or nature.

Then listen for sounds that are near you
for another few minutes.

These sounds might be noises in the room
you're in or just outside the door.

Lastly, listen for sounds that are inside you
for few more minutes.

You might listen to your breath
or your belly grumbling.

If your mind wanders, don't worry;
just come back to listening
for sounds around you.

Finger Tap

Sit comfortably with your palms up,
resting on your knees.

Each time you take a deep inhale and deep exhale,
tap your thumb to a finger,
starting with your index finger.

Move to the middle finger, the ring finger,
and lastly, the pinky finger.

Then start over from the index finger,
matching your breath to the finger taps.

Continue in this way for at least five minutes.

51

Happy Place

Take a moment to breathe deeply,
until you are inhaling for four counts
and exhaling for four counts.

As you are sitting silently,
start to visualize your "happy place."

This could be a special place in nature,
like a forest or ocean,
or any other place where
you feel safe and happy.

Imagine this place—
what it looks like,
what you see,
and what you hear.

You might even imagine
people who are with you.

Breathing deeply,
take yourself on an imaginary journey
to your favorite place.

Light a Candle

Light your favorite candle and place it
on the ground or on the table in front of you.

Come to sitting comfortably,
place your palms up on your knees,
and roll your shoulders down your back.

As you inhale and exhale for four counts each,
watch the flicker of the flame.

Let your eyelids grow heavy and
narrow your focus on the candle.

If your mind wanders,
let go of your thoughts and
come back to watching the flame.

Continue like this,
gazing at the flame and breathing deeply,
for at least five minutes.

Loving-Kindness

Take a deep breath in and then
exhale slowly for three to five counts.

On an exhale, think of filling yourself with love.

Imagine the warm color red
enveloping your body.

On the next exhale,
think of sending love and kindness
to someone close to you.

Then on the next exhale,
think of sending loving kindness
to someone you are having a difficult
relationship with at the moment.

Then send love and kindness out
to the world around you—
the animals, the trees,
your neighbors, and your city.

Lastly, send out love and kindness to the world.

Finish your loving-kindness meditation
by coming back to breathing naturally.

Mandala Beads

Come to sitting cross-legged
on a blanket or bolster.

Breathe naturally.

Place a mandala bead necklace or bracelet
in your right hand and close your eyes.

Breathe deeply, counting to four
as you inhale and exhale.

Each time you take in a deep inhale,
pull your thumb down across one bead.

Continue like this with every inhale and exhale
by moving your thumb around the beads.

Some mandala necklaces have a knot and thread,
so you'll know when you've been once around.
You could stop after one turn around
or keep going to do two rounds.

Continue with your five-count breathing
while focusing on moving around the beads.

59

Nature Seat

Go outside to find a comfortable position.

You may like to sit in your favorite nature spot,
even if you have to drive there.

Take a moment to get settled and
bring your attention to your breath.

Start your breathing practice,
listening to the sounds around you.

With each breath,
take in the beauty of nature and
completely relax your body.

Sweet Smells

Put some essential oil in your diffuser
or sit next to some fresh-cut flowers.

You might even sit in your kitchen
while you have something delicious
baking in the oven.

Whatever scent you choose,
try to find something sweet smelling.

Close your eyes and get comfortable,
wherever you are.

Take a few moments to breathe deeply
and focus on the aroma around you.

Think positive thoughts
every time you inhale.

Tension Release

Come to lying down or sitting
in an easy position with a tall spine.

Breathe deeply.

Start at your toes.
Tense your toes and then release them.

Next, tense your calves and then release.

Work up your body,
tensing your muscles and
then releasing any tension.

Move up to your knees,
upper legs, belly, chest,
hands, and arms.

Then continue to your shoulders,
chin, cheeks, nose, and forehead.

Then spend a few moments scanning your body
to release any leftover tension.

Send healing thoughts to each part
of your body that needs it.

Breathe and relax.

Three People

Once you're settled into a comfortable position
in a quiet place, breathe naturally.

Bring three people to your mind.

As you inhale and exhale for at least five minutes,
let those three people linger in your mind.

Send them good thoughts.

Send them gratitude.

Send them happiness and good health.

Think about ways to build a stronger connection
with these people in your life.

Let your mind wander to
creative and generous ideas.

Tip of Your Nose

Sit comfortably with a tall spine
and close your eyes.

While you are breathing deeply in and out,
bring your focus to your nose,
looking gently toward its tip.

Or you could instead focus on the space
under your nose where your breath
comes in and out and feel the sensation
of your breath there.

If your mind wanders, don't worry,
simply come back to focusing on
your breath at your nose.

Continue like this for at least five minutes.

Your Favorite Thing

Stop for a moment and
sit in a comfortable position.

Place something special in your left hand.

It could be a gem, stone, trinket,
or something that means a lot to you.

As you meditate, think about why
that item is special to you.

For example, pretend you have a rock
painted with "gratitude" on it.

Think of all the ways you are
grateful with each breath.

More Products by Giselle Shardlow

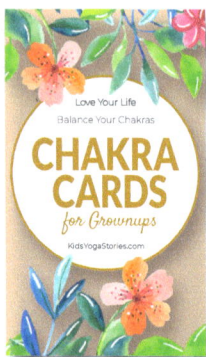

Chakra Cards
for Grownups

Positive Affirmation Cards
for Grownups

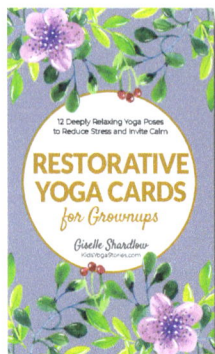

Restorative Yoga Cards
for Grownups

Monthly Yoga Challenges

Buy now at www.KidsYogaStories.com/store

Find us here:

giselle@kidsyogastories.com
www.pinterest.com/kidsyogastories
www.instagram.com/kidsyogastories
www.facebook.com/kidsyogastories
www.twitter.com/kidsyogastories
www.amazon.com/author/giselleshardlow
www.goodreads.com/giselleshardlow

KIDS YOGA STORIES

www.ingramcontent.com/pod-product-compliance
Lightning Source LLC
Chambersburg PA
CBHW040035110426
42741CB00031B/104